CO-APM-648

ALCOHOL
IN
AMERICA
THE
PRICE
WE PAY

ALCOHOLISM & DRUG ABUSE INSTITUTE
UNIVERSITY OF WASHINGTON
3937 - 15th AVENUE N.E., NL-15
SEATTLE, WASHINGTON 98105

ALCOHOL
IN
AMERICA
THE
PRICE
WE PAY

by **Rashi Fein**
Foreword by Walter Heller

CareInstitute
Newport Beach, California

© 1984 by CareInstitute
All rights reserved.
Published in the United States by CareInstitute.
Reproduction in whole or part, in any form, including storage in memory device system, is forbidden without written permission . . . except that portions may be used in broadcast or printed commentary or review when fully attributed to author and publication by names.

Library of Congress Catalog No. 84-70989. ISBN 0-917877-00-4
Requests for additional copies should be addressed to
CareInstitute, in care of
CompCare Publications
P.O. Box 27777
Minneapolis, Minnesota 55427

Contents

CareInstitute
An Introduction

CareInstitute is a non-profit, public service organization dedicated to research and education in the field of behavioral medicine.

The general purpose of CareInstitute is to advance public and professional understanding of behavioral medicine problems and issues through educational programs, seminars and workshops; through professional monographs and publications; and through applied research. CareInstitute's founder, Comprehensive Care Corporation, is the nation's largest private provider of chemical dependency treatment services.

Most of CareInstitute's projects to date have focused on the area of alcoholism and drug abuse treatment. These projects have included a nationwide study of medical complications and polydrug disorders among patients seeking help for chemical dependence; an independent analysis of insurance coverage for alcoholism treatment; and an educational program for physicians on the diagnosis and treatment of alcoholism.

This study, the most recent CareInstitute publication, was generated out of an intense and controversial debate during the past several years regarding the economics of providing alcoholism treatment to Americans. Many voices have joined the din — providers, insurers, health care professionals, lawmakers, cost-benefit accountants, recovering alcoholics themselves, even the national media. One vital group has been conspicuous in its absence from the fray, however: economists. Noted Harvard economist Dr. Rashi Fein sets out to rectify that absence in this volume, addressing the difficult and complicated economic and social issues surrounding alcohol abuse and its treatment in a bold, original light. His important economic analysis of the factors involved makes clear, persuasive arguments for a completely new national agenda on America's drinking problems.

Simply stated, Dr. Fein asks and then answers the essential question — what is the cost to America of *not* treating alcoholism?

Foreword

As one of the leading authorities on medical economics, and as a member of the Harvard Medical School faculty, Dr. Rashi Fein is singularly well qualified to analyze the economics of alcoholism. In this analysis, drawing on both governmental and private studies, he documents in unmistakable fashion the staggering costs of alcoholism and the nation's costly underfunding of efforts to control and cure it.

The conclusion from his careful appraisal is crystal clear: given the huge direct and indirect costs inflicted on society by alcohol abusers and the huge benefits that flow from education, research, prevention, treatment and rehabilitation in this field, the country needs to invest more, not less, in this undertaking, needs to stop being penny-wise and pound-foolish.

This may not be a popular message at a time when cost containment is the order of the day in health care. But that is precisely why Dr. Fein's study of the *economics* of alcohol abuse is so timely and important. Purely in terms of cost-effectiveness—in terms of the large potential return per dollar invested—his study shows that it would be false economy to hold outlays on alcoholism treatment to their present levels, let alone, to cut them back. That would be a prime case of confusing parsimony with economy.

What drives this point home is Dr. Fein's convincing argument that enlarged investment in alcohol treatment could actually shrink overall health care cost. Alcohol abuse often lies at the root of other diseases—of the liver, the pancreas, the heart, the central nervous system, and so on. As he puts it, "Even the narrowest economic accounting indicates that it [investment in alcohol treatment] more than pays for itself in reductions of other health care costs."

When the cost-benefit net is widened to embrace the damaging impact on the heavy drinker's productivity and widened further to include the alcohol-caused carnage on the highways, the fires, crimes, drownings and suicides attributable to alcohol, Dr. Fein concludes that the costs of alcohol abuse are nine times the treatment costs broadly conceived. If only the costs of treatment of alcoholism as such are counted, the ratio is much higher.

Although the cost estimates he cites and presents are, by their nature, approximations, they seem to have been made conservatively. Still, he underscores the need for more work on the economic dimension of the alcoholism problem. Updating of the data, more intensive analysis of secondary and tertiary costs, comparisons of the cost-effectiveness of alternative forms of treatment, more precise appraisals of the higher health care costs for problem drinkers—these are just a few of the challenging economic issues that call for further research.

But for health policymakers who need to take a comprehensive, a macroeconomic, view of the role of alcoholism treatment in America's health delivery system, Rashi Fein has already provided invaluable guidance in this illuminating study.

Walter W. Heller
Regents' Professor of Economics
University of Minnesota

A distinguished economist, academician, and civil servant, Professor Heller served as chairman of the President's Council of Economic Advisors from 1961 to 1964 and is currently a consultant to the Congressional Budget Office. In addition Dr. Heller is a member of the Time *Board of Economists and the Board of Contributors of the* Wall Street Journal.

Acknowledgments

In 1957 I undertook to write a monograph on the economics of mental illness. I found the task intellectually stimulating and rewarding. Recalling that challenge, I accepted Dr. Edward Carels' invitation, some twenty-five years later, to examine the economic dimensions of alcoholism in the United States. The American health care delivery and financing system had changed greatly over the quarter of a century since I last addressed the economics of a specific disease. It is, therefore, not surprising that I found this latest effort equally stimulating and especially so since it provided an opportunity to consider the implications of those changes on the climate within which health policy is developed.

I must express my gratitude to those who assisted me in this endeavor, without whose offer to help I would not have dared to undertake this task and without whose efforts I would not have been able to complete it. Dr. Carels and Arline Kaplan provided entree into the literature on alcoholism and reduced the scope of my own research and bibliographic effort substantially. In addition they enhanced both the substance and readability of the manuscript by their own research—most especially by comparing the economic dimensions of alcoholism and other diseases—and by their careful editorial review. I hope they are as pleased with my efforts as I with theirs.

I should also note that ours has been a happy relationship. I have, as I would have expected, been given free reign to look at the data and reach my own conclusions. The data tell a shocking story, one that calls for action. I can only hope that those who read this manuscript will agree and that, collectively, we will press for an appropriate response to the economic dimensions of alcoholism.

Rashi Fein
Harvard University
1984

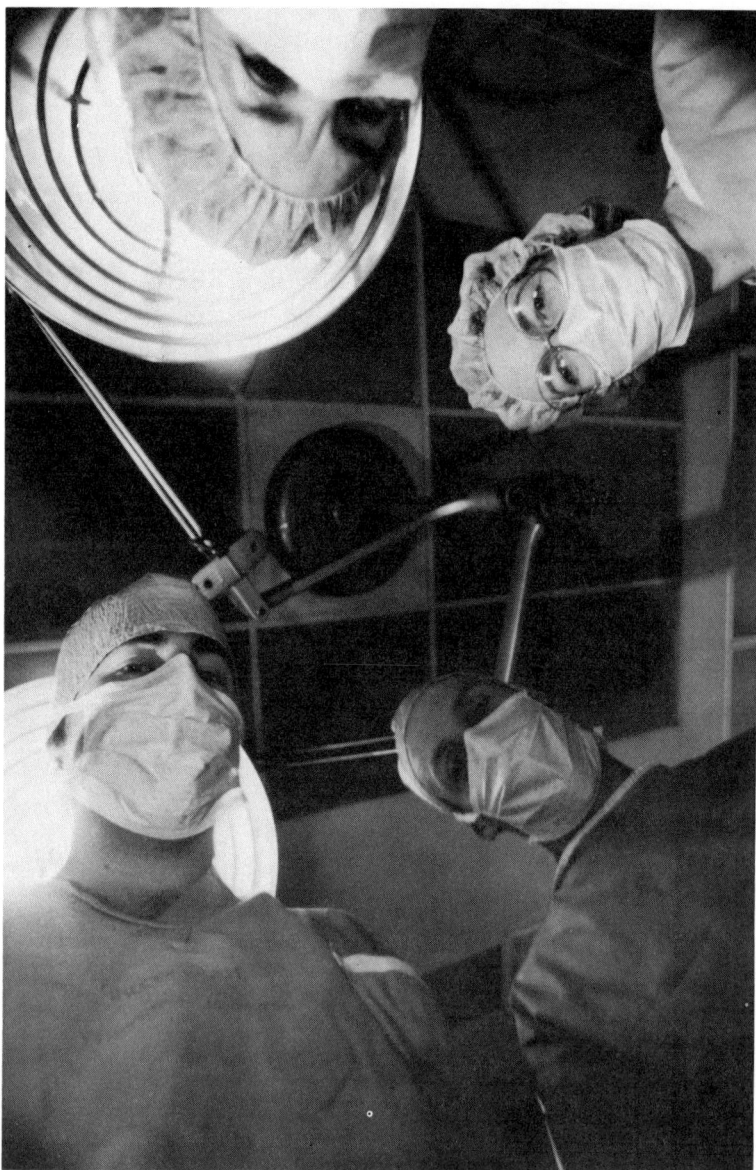

© *Marv Wolf/After-Image*

1

Health Care in America
An Economic Overview

In the early 1940s medical news vied with war news, as penicillin worked one unbelievable miracle after another. In the mid-fifties a simple cry heralded another achievement in medical history: "It works!" Polio vaccine was ready to march against the dread disease. The late sixties saw Dr. Christiaan Barnard become a popular international hero for his Olympian achievement in heart surgery. And in somber contrast to these dramatic advances in medicine and medical treatment, a riptide had been steadily swelling on another equally devastating disease. By 1980 four hundred thousand people each year were being caught in the undertow of alcoholism, abusing the substance and themselves until they became medically diagnosable as alcoholics or problem drinkers. Today the total is estimated at almost fifteen million Americans.

Although news reporting and educational efforts in various media have raised the collective American consciousness of the increasing prevalence and impact of alcoholism, still the problem grows ever greater, both in terms of the number of lives affected directly and indirectly and the economic costs.

In spite of important successes in the treatment of this disease, alcoholism remains one of the nation's largest and most complicated health problems due to the cross currents of social and economic issues. To begin to understand why, one must look at not only the disease itself, but also at the complexity of the American medical enterprise and alcoholism's place in it.

The American health sector is a labyrinthine mixture of overlapping private and public financing mechanisms, delivery systems, and operating programs. It contains profit and not-for-profit entities as well as competitive and monopolistic elements. Its special characteristics have evolved over an extended period of time in response to fluctuating attitudes toward disease and its prevention, advances in medical knowledge, rising levels of economic well-being, and changes in the structure of the urban American society.

In the period following World War II, public and private action was molded by an expansionary spirit. This was the era of advances in biomedicine and science, growth in capital investment in hospitals, and enlargement in the number of and enrollment in medical schools. Importantly, it was the time when private health insurance and, in the latter 1960s, Medicare and Medicaid made it possible for more Americans to obtain the benefits of modern medicine.

Given the multiple sources of financial support for medical education and research and payment for medical care services; given the mix of private and public organizations that delivered care; given the traditional American aversion to central direction; the health sector grew without a master plan.

The federal government acted and reacted in the face of changing medical care priorities without developing a comprehensive and consistent health policy. Yet, neither the federal government nor the various states were prepared to give free reign to the market as the allocative device, that is, to permit the production and distribution of health care without regard to social and national needs and to equity considerations.

Thus, a mixture of government planning and market forces, influenced both by consumer and producer perceptions of need, helped mold the health care structure and determine the health care issues that we face today. Among these issues are questions of priority and of costs:

(1) Do the priorities set by medical researchers, educators, providers (including both practicing physicians and health care institutions), patients, and third-party payers reflect the total social and economic impact of the prevailing diseases?

(2) If access to health care is guaranteed, so price is no longer a central factor in decisions about the delivery and use of services, what control mechanisms will be necessary to guard against a continuing escalation of costs, prices, and expenditures?

These two issues have an operational interrelationship. In other words, the priorities awarded diseases in terms of the training of physicians, biomedical research, the practices of acute-care institutions, and the characteristics of third-party payments affect costs and expenditures. In turn, efforts to control costs inevitably affect and influence priorities; that is, he who pays the piper calls the tune. There is little reason to expect that the needs and desires of the numerous decision makers, each with his own objectives and reward systems, will yield a set of health care priorities that reflect the various, sometimes conflicting, criteria that might appropriately be used to determine how many and where the dollars should be spent.

The last point — and the two questions posed earlier — suggest the striking difference between the health care system and most other sectors of the economy. In areas in which society is prepared to leave production and allocation decisions to the market and in which government's role is to help ensure that the market operates in a competitive environment, there is little reason to ask those kinds of questions. Priorities and the level of expenditures, presumably, reflect consumer choices and decisions (though, of course, the latter are influenced by advertising and producer behavior).

Health care, however, is viewed as an area in which the market should not reign supreme. Health care is seen as a different kind of good or service. In response to that difference, our society, like other societies, has responded by developing its own set of programs and interventions.

These efforts, in turn, create their own problems and challenges. That, however, is not to be deplored. These challenges are the natural side effects or by-products of the actions taken in rejecting what society believes would create an even larger difficulty: rationing health care only to those who can afford it.

That type of rationing would be an affront to many, if not most, Americans. Furthermore, it would inevitably have a stultifying effect on the quality of the American medical enterprise. Without government and philanthropic dollars that help support the education of America's physicians and much of the nation's biomedical research, the number of new discoveries, developments, and technologies would decrease, thus affecting not only those who couldn't afford care, but persons of higher income as well. Also, because modern medicine involves substantial capital and overhead costs, some services would no longer be available because their per unit cost of production would become extravagantly high while other services would decline in quality because personnel and facilities would become "rusty" from lack of practice. In short, in this kind of system all of us would suffer. Thus, the desire to increase access to care is based both on altruism and self-interest.

The existing institutional arrangements of America's health sector force us to ask a set of questions which need not be asked in most other areas of economic endeavor: do health care expenditures bear "appropriate" relation to the benefits of the associated health services? Do producer, consumer, and insurer motivations force the health system to ever-increasing levels of expenditures— expenditures which may be higher compared to other societal needs, than are warranted? Without the controls exerted by the market or by tight budget and spending limits imposed by the various funding mechanisms, is it inevitable that America's expenditures on health care, from all sources, be unnecessarily high?

If it is ultimately true that aggregate health care costs are higher than is appropriate, it does not necessarily follow that this is also the case for all health conditions or in all parts of the health sector. In an era in which society is preoccupied with finding ways to limit total health care expenditures, it is easy for public and private sector decision makers at all levels to ignore or forget the fact that not all parts or activities of the health care system are overfunded. Unilateral reductions in spending can hit with devastating force those health conditions which have historically suffered from relative neglect, yet whose impact has been underestimated.

Spending too little rather than too much for the treatment of a particular disease, such as mental illness or alcoholism, often occurs:

- if stigma is attached to a particular illness and thus to seeking care;

- if the illness is not easily detected;

- if the illness is believed to be incurable or curable outside the mainstream of medicine in a less costly fashion;

- if the illness is associated with behavior patterns and a lifestyle that most people attack on moral grounds, so that the illness is viewed as retribution, and curing it is seen as encouraging the "wrong" kind of behavior;

- if most physicians and other health care professionals are disinterested in researching or treating the illness, and those who are interested are not accorded status from their colleagues;

- if treatment is labor rather than capital intensive, requiring payment for staff time rather than costly medical technology;

- if the condition does not fall neatly into the normal departmental structure of a medical school, hospital or medical specialty;

- if prevention or successful treatment of the disease requires social as well as medical intervention and a collective sustained effort by a number of disciplines;

- if third-party payers view coverage for the disease as optional rather than necessary.

In our society, health-spending decisions are made via numerous uncoordinated large and small, individual and collective, political and economic, non-market and market influences. The decisions are further influenced by tradition, tastes and bias, and by economic and political variables as well. Thus, whatever our views on the aggregate level of health expenditures, we are forced to ask whether we are likely to be spending too much or too little on research, prevention, and treatment for a particular disease.

At present, the ubiquitous concern about rising health care costs is dictating many and varied changes in the health care delivery system. The press of cost containment is everywhere. In this environment, virtually any suggestion that appears to reduce hospitalization or health care utilization is embraced with interest. Because alcoholism treatment has only recently gained entrance into the medical mainstream, treatment for this disease has had to face a host of cost benefit and cost effectiveness questions in its quest for parity with other major diseases. The question we hope to answer throughout the remainder of this book is: "Does America spend too much or too little on the prevention, research, and treatment of alcoholism?"

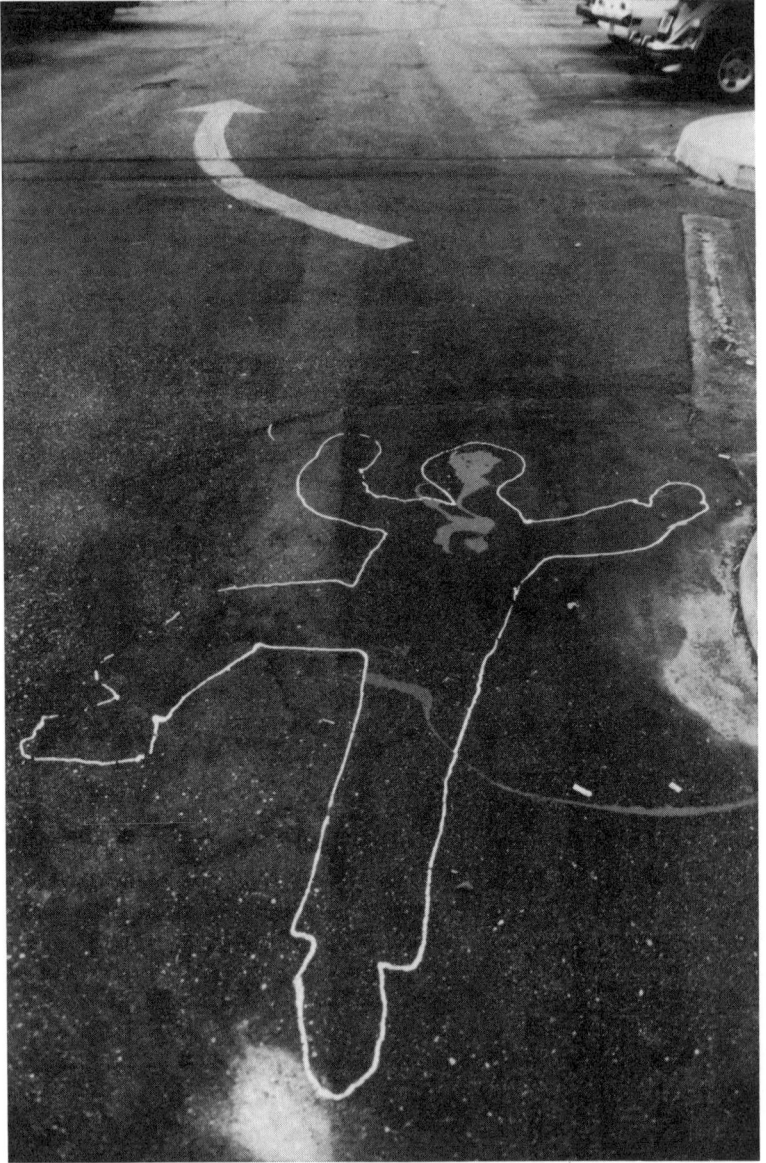

© *Marv Wolf/After-Image*

2

Alcohol Abuse
A National Problem

Alcoholism was identified in the 1950s as a disease by the American Medical Association, the World Health Organization, and other health care organizations.[1] But, until the last few years, its acceptance as a disease and as a national public health problem had been slow. Indeed, the concept of the skid row, irredeemable, morally derelict alcoholic still filters into our thinking. In one study, 41 percent of the respondents agreed that to be known as an alcoholic would destroy a person's reputation, and 45 percent believed treatment should be administered away from one's neighborhood to assure privacy.[2]

The stigma occurs among health care professionals as well. A survey of the Michigan Academy of Family Physicians asked physicians to list five medical conditions which they disliked.[3] More than half (55.8 percent) cited alcoholism and alcohol abuse. Authors Lewis and Sheps in their recent book, *The Sick Citadel: The American Academic Medical Center and the Public Interest*, observe that "the educational program (of the medical center) is dominated by the choices made in research and patient care which reflect the interests of the many specialized individuals and groups that make up the faculty."[4] They note that this creates a "mismatch between the health needs of the public and what is concentrated upon, demonstrated, and taught in our academic medical centers" and conclude that "geriatrics and alcoholism present massive problems which get little, if any, attention in the academic medical center." The question they ask is, "How can this experience be thought to prepare students adequately for medical practice?"

Recent polls indicate that the public may be more sensitive to alcohol problems than are many health care providers. The responses obtained in a specially commissioned 1982 Gallup poll are striking:[5]

- Eighty-one percent of Americans believe that alcohol abuse is a major national problem.

- On an average, one out of three Americans reports that drinking has been a cause of trouble in his/her own family; among those aged fifty and older, one of four reports family drinking problems; and among eighteen to twenty-four-year olds, the ratio rises to two out of five.

- Four out of five Americans agree that alcoholism is a disease which should be treated in a hospital. This figure has risen substantially from 63 percent in 1955 to 79 percent in 1982.

- Almost three out of five (59 percent) said alcoholism treatment should be covered by medical insurance *the same as any other disease*. (emphasis added)

A large majority of the public thus perceives alcoholism as a major national problem and as a disease. The fact that one out of three respondents reported alcoholism has been a source of trouble in the family indicates that alcoholism is not an abstraction, but a disease that many have encountered.

Furthermore, federal officials and agencies have expressed their concern with alcoholism (and with alcohol and drug abuse) on a number of occasions and in a variety of ways:

- The Congressional Office of Technology Assessment in its 1983 report on *The Effectiveness and Costs of Alcoholism Treatment* noted that "the problems of alcoholism and alcohol abuse are too serious in terms of their impact on the Nation, for the problem to be ignored." The report noted alcoholism may be responsible for up to 15 percent of the Nation's health care costs and for significantly lowering the productivity of workers at all strata of the economic system...Alcoholism and alcohol abuse also adversely affect the health, social relations, psychological well-being and economic status of a large number of individuals."[6]

- A United States Surgeon General, Julius B. Richmond, reported that alcohol is a contributing factor in more than 10 percent of all deaths in the United States.[7]

- Dr. William Mayer, while administrator of the Alcohol, Drug Abuse and Mental Health Administration, noted that "ten thousand young people are killed every year in highway accidents involving alcohol, the leading cause of death in the sixteen to twenty-four age group. I personally believe that this continuing carnage should give every citizen serious pause, considering that it took only 200 deaths a year in the 1950s for the Nation to declare polio an epidemic."[8]

- *The Federal Strategy for Prevention of Drug Abuse and Drug Trafficking 1982* called for a "comprehensive program to reduce drug and alcohol abuse in the United States." It urged continued integration of drug and alcohol services into the general health care system, expansion of alcohol and drug treatment services by the private sector and expansion of third-party payments for the treatment of alcoholism.[9]

These perceptions of alcoholism as a growing national problem are supported by alarming social statistics.

Prevalence of Alcohol Abuse

- An estimated 14.7 million Americans suffer from alcoholism or problem drinking and their numbers are increasing by 0.4 million a year.[10,11]

- A 1983 survey sponsored by the National Institute of Mental Health revealed that 13.6 percent of all adults have experienced clinically significant alcohol abuse or dependence in their lifetime — making alcohol abuse/dependence the most prevalent lifetime disorder of all forms of mental disorders.[12]

• One out of five teenagers between the ages of fourteen and seventeen is estimated to be a problem drinker.[13]

Certainly, alcoholism and alcohol abuse are not "low grade" afflictions — conditions which affect individuals only as minor irritants with negative effects which can generally and easily be dealt with or ignored.

Deaths

Alcoholism and alcohol abuse are this nation's fourth leading cause of death accounting for more than 127,385 premature deaths each year.[14,15,16]

• The United States has one of the highest rates of automobile accidents involving alcohol in the world. Each day, 71 people are killed and 2,000 people are injured in alcohol-related accidents.[17]

• Up to 68 percent of the people who drown, 50 percent of those who die in falling accidents and 50 percent of those adults killed in fires had been drinking.[18]

- The rate of suicide among alcoholics is as much as 30 times that of the general population.[19]

The listing below provides a measure of the extent of alcohol-related deaths.[20]

Alcohol Dependence Syndrome	4,350
Alcohol Abuse (nondependent)	889
Cirrhosis-Alcohol Mention	9,166
Alcoholic Cardiomyopathy	650
Alcohol Poisoning	385
Alcoholic Psychosis	454
Alcoholic Gastritis	84
Alcoholic Polyneuropathy	4
Cancer of Liver	3,146
(56 percent of 5,618)	
Cirrhosis of Liver and Chronic Liver Disease	9,551
(44.6 percent of 21,417)	
Respiratory Tuberculosis	405
(25 percent of 1621)	
Acute Pancreatitis	1,008
(35.5 percent of 2,840)	
Homicides	21,121
(87 percent of 24,278)	
Suicides	21,495
(80 percent of 26,869)	
Motor Vehicle Accidents	27,317
(59 percent of 46,300)	
Fire	2,911
(50 percent of 5,822)	
Drownings	4,109
(68 percent of 6,043)	
Falls	6,647
(50 percent of 13,294)	
Other Accidents	13,693
(50 percent of 27,387)	

Disease

Alcohol abuse is a significant factor in some thirty diseases, including hypertension, gastritis, pancreatitis, and various forms of cancer. The American Hospital Association in its 1983 Policy and Statement declared that alcoholism and drug abuse problems contribute "significantly to a variety of medical complications" and "are seen in as many as 50 percent of the patients admitted to hospitals with other diagnoses."[21]
Several research studies have been conducted to determine the number of hospital patients who are alcohol abusers.[22] The proportions vary, depending upon the treatment offered and the population served. A study at Harlem Hospital with a high concentration of poor patients found 60 percent of the men and 34 percent of the women were alcoholics. A 1981 survey of patients at Montrose Veterans Administration hospital in New York disclosed that 45 percent of the inpatients were alcoholics or problem drinkers. At a hospital in Anaheim, California, 32 percent of the patients were considered to be either alcoholics or possible alcoholics. A review of studies done in several hospitals finds that about 20 percent of people hospitalized for other medical conditions may be alcoholics. A total of 1,004 patients in seven hospitals in the Minneapolis and St. Paul area were screened for potential alcoholism. Approximately 20 percent of the patients surfaced as being alcoholics or problem drinkers.[23] A group of twenty-nine alcoholism treatment experts working in nine different settings was asked to estimate the percentage of all hospital beds occupied by alcoholics. The average of their estimates was 22.5 percent.[24] Bayer in his review of the literature shows a range of alcohol abusers in the inpatient population from

8.7 percent to 47 percent depending upon the criteria used for defining alcohol abuse.[25] Based upon these studies, one may conclude that at least one out of every five patients in a general hospital is an alcoholic or problem drinker.

Eckardt et. al. in the *Journal of the American Medical Association* discussed the multiple health hazards associated with alcohol consumption, some of which are described below:[26]

- "Alcoholism has been associated with a number of adverse effects on the cardiovascular system, including a specific cardiomyopathy, low mean cardiac output, and depressed myocardial contractility. The drinking of large amounts of alcohol is associated with significant increases in blood pressure."

- "Heavy drinking increases the risk of cancer developing in the tongue, mouth, hypopharynx, oropharynx, esophagus, larynx, and liver."

- "Fetal Alcohol Syndrome (FAS) has been identified among some children of alcoholic women...It has been suggested that FAS is one of the leading causes of birth defects associated with mental retardation. Short of the full complement of defects that characterize FAS, heavy alcohol use by women has been associated with birth anomalies."

- "Alcohol abuse plays a major role in such liver diseases as fatty liver, alcoholic hepatitis, and cirrhosis of the liver."

- "Heavy alcohol intake contributes to nutritional deficiency by disrupting physiological and metabolic processes of digestion."

- "Long-term alcoholism, especially when combined with malnutrition often results in severe neurological and cognitive deficits" (e.g., Wernicke-Korsakoff syndrome).

- "Both pneumonia and tuberculosis appear frequently among alcoholics."

- "There are known alcohol-related endocrinologic and sexual dysfunctions in male alcoholics, with or without overt liver disease... Recent case studies of women and basic research in female animals suggest that alcohol may induce early postmenopausal amenorrhea or even ovarian failure..."

A review of the literature also indicates that alcoholism is associated with significant increases in the utilization of medical care services for alcohol-related (but not alcohol-specific) conditions.[27] A Pennsylvania cost containment program involving 311,000 employees found that alcoholics and substance abusers use eight times more hospital days than all other subscribers for illnesses other than their addiction, and 70 percent of these other illnesses are related to or caused by their substance abuse problem.[28]

Social Costs

Beyond the health consequences of alcoholism, there are the social costs:

- 40 percent divorce rate among families experiencing alcohol problems.[29]

- 5.7 million cases a year of family violence linked to alcohol abuse.[30]

- 3.4 million arrests annually linked to alcohol and drug abuse violations.[31]

- 25 to 50 percent loss in productivity among alcoholic employees.[32,33]

Many of the medical complications and social problems develop because the underlying alcoholism problem goes undetected or untreated. Joseph Califano, former secretary of the Department of Health, Education, and Welfare, in a report to the governor of New York, explained: "A careful look behind the diagnostic charts reveals that many of our general hospitals are overwhelmed by patients with alcohol-related problems. Yet, most of these patients are not formally identified as alcoholics or problem drinkers."[34] He notes that as many as two-thirds of the alcoholics and problem drinkers seen in New York's hospital emergency rooms are not identified as having an alcohol problem. The National Institute on Alcohol Abuse and Alcoholism notes that approximately 85 percent of this nation's alcoholics and problem drinkers are not receiving any formal treatment for their disease.[35] And the 1982 National Drug and

Alcoholism Treatment Utilization Survey reveals that the number of alcoholism treatment units has decreased by 5 percent within two years and the number of clients served dropped between 3.5 and 6 percent, depending on the setting.[36]

© *Peter Garfield/After-Image*

3

The Economics of Alcoholism
Direct and Indirect Costs

The human costs of alcoholism and alcohol abuse are massive both for the abusers and those whose lives are indirectly affected. In addition to the pain and suffering from alcoholism and alcohol abuse, severe economic costs are generated that spread beyond the individual and his or her family to the greater economy. These are costs that all of us bear.

In studying the economic impact of disease, economists have found it useful to divide costs into two components: direct and indirect. Direct costs are the costs of treatment, including prevention and other efforts to mitigate the impact of the particular ailment and its sequelae. Indirect costs are the costs that result from the loss of productive effort as a consequence of the ravages of the particular ailment (including, therefore, such costs as arise from lower productivity on the job, work absences, and premature death).

Increased expenditures on prevention and treatment reduce pain and suffering. Importantly, if treatment or prevention is successful, the increase in direct costs which deal with the ailment may reduce the indirect costs of the disease. Thus direct costs — as in many areas of social and economic activity, for example, in education — have both a consumption and an investment component. They yield increases in satisfaction and quality of life and can be considered as consumption. They also yield increases in production and thus can be thought of as an investment.

The potential inverse relationship between direct and indirect costs cannot be overstressed. The national economy, and all of us who share in its product, bear the indirect costs of illness. Although these costs in many cases exceed the direct costs of the disease, they are not included in the various compilations of National Health Expenditures, for they represent what we as a nation lose, not what we spend. Yet, this omission has an unfortunate corollary: the presence of indirect costs (and their relationship to direct costs) is often completely overlooked. As a consequence, there may be pressures to cut expenditures (at the extreme, not to finance various kinds of treatment) without adequate consideration of the possible impact of such actions on indirect costs. Put simply, there may be pressures to under-invest in some aspects of medical care, due in part to a faulty analytic framework which understates the total economic costs of disease and the investment return (and which often ignores the human and social implications as well).

That the direct costs of alcoholism and alcohol abuse are large (though we shall have to consider what "large" means and to what it might be related) is clear and well known. Difficult as it is to allocate all costs appropriately, it is nevertheless possible to estimate the direct costs of alcoholism and alcohol abuse treatment.

Several economists have estimated the total economic costs to America of alcohol abuse and alcoholism. These estimates were built on different assumptions, but they dramatize the magnitude of costs and the impact which alcohol consumption has on the American economy. The results of two major studies will be discussed in detail. The reader is cautioned that comparisons between them are difficult because of the different assumptions and analytic approaches used in deriving the estimates. For example, direct and indirect costs are not calculated in the same way for both studies. The reader is asked to focus on the global or macroeconomic aspects of the data and not the individual components. The point to be made is there are many large and unforeseen economic consequences associated with alcohol abuse. Indirect costs are most frequently ignored when consideration is given to paying for the direct costs of treatment. They are also rarely considered when cost containment programs are implemented.

Berry, Boland, Smart, and Kanak, in a report for the National Insitute on Alcohol Abuse and Alcoholism, estimated that alcoholism and alcohol misuse cost the United States approximately $43 billion in 1975, or nearly $78 billion in 1983 dollars.[37] Table 1 presents the costs calculated in six major categories: lost production, health and medical care, motor vehicle accidents, violent crime, social responses, and fire losses. When analyzing the costs, two perspectives were kept in mind. First, because problem drinking often makes people less functional, society loses part of the economic value of normal production. Second, because certain goods and services, such as health and social service resources and police protection, have to be increased to cope with some of the consequences of alcohol abuse, the added costs must be paid for by the general public.

Table 1
ECONOMIC COSTS OF ALCOHOL MISUSE
AND ALCOHOLISM

($ in millions)		1975	1983 equivalent
Lost production:		$19,640	$35,744
Lost market production-men	$15,460		
Lost military production	410		
Premature mortality	3,770		
Health and medical:		$12,740	$23,186
Hospital care	8,400		
Physician's services	1,300		
Other health services........	2,090		
Research, training, etc.	950		
Motor vehicle accidents:		$ 5,140	$ 9,355
Violent crime:		$ 2,860	$ 5,205
Social responses:		$ 1,940	$ 3,531
Workman's compensation, public assistance, welfare..	1,300		
Treatment...............	54		
Research and training.....	20.7		
Alcohol treatment	74.7		
Highway safety	29.2		
Fire protection	392		
Fire:		$ 430	$ 783
TOTAL ECONOMIC COSTS		**$42,750**	**$77,804**

SOURCE: Data from Ralph Berry, James Boland, Charles Smart, and James Kanak, *The Economic Costs of Alcohol Abuse and Alcoholism 1975.* Report prepared for National Institute on Alcohol Abuse and Alcoholism under Contract No. ADM 281-76-0016. 1977.

The largest economic cost of alcohol abuse and alcoholism was the $19.6 billion accounted for by lost production of goods and services. Health and medical care represented the second largest component of total costs, $12.74 billion. But these costs were associated with *alcohol-related* illnesses, such as certain cancers, pneumonia, stomach and duodenal ulcers, cirrhosis of the liver, etc. The $12.74 billion category does not include the actual costs of treating alcoholism specifically. These costs, listed under "social responses" on Table 1 were estimated at only $74.7 million.

Analyzing the data from Berry et. al., one sees how little was spent on alcoholism rehabilitation efforts compared to the amount spent on treating the health consequences of alcohol abuse and compared to the amount lost to this nation through lost productivity. For example, the amount spent for alcoholism treatment and rehabilitation per se was $54 million with an additional $20.7 million for research and training. That $74.7 million is the equivalent of 0.6 percent of the $12.7 billion spent on treating alcohol-related medical problems. Furthermore, the $74.7 million is the equivalent of 0.4 percent of the $19.6 billion in lost production.

Another in-depth analysis of alcohol-related costs to society was published in 1981. Cruze and Associates at the Research Triangle Institute prepared a report in which they estimated the costs of alcohol consumption to the United States.[38] The estimate was $49.37 billion for 1977. Table 2 shows two categories: "core costs—direct and indirect costs" and "other related costs."

Note that of the total $49.37 billion in costs (in 1977 dollars), nearly $36.8 billion is indirect costs, that is, costs associated with lost productivity due to premature mortality, reduced productivity, lost work time, and lost employment.

Those indirect costs break down as follows: the indirect economic cost of mortality due to alcohol abuse was $10.7 billion. Nearly $7 billion of that was accounted for by alcohol-related deaths in motor vehicle crashes, homicides, falls, or fires. The indirect economic losses associated with morbidity due to alcohol abuse were $26.1 billion with more than 90 percent accounted for by reduced productivity. The other related indirect costs of alcoholism included $1.4 billion due to lost productivity because of alcohol abusers being incarcerated and $0.4 billion due to others losing worktime from motor vehicle crashes.

TABLE 2
ECONOMIC COSTS TO SOCIETY
OF ALCOHOL ABUSE

($ in millions)		1977	1983 equivalent
Core Costs			
Direct:			
Treatment..................		$ 5,637	$ 9,425
Alcohol abuse treated in specialty settings.....	$ 707		
Alcohol-related illness and trauma............	$4,930		
Support (research, education, training, construction, insurance administration)		735	1,229
Indirect:			
Premature mortality......		10,715	17,916
Morbidity resulting in.....		26,074	43,596
Reduced productivity, Lost work time........	$23,593		
Lost employment.......	$ 2,481		
Total Core Costs		$43,161	$72,166
Other Related Costs			
Direct:			
Motor vehicle crashes (funeral, legal/court, etc.)....................		$ 1,782	$ 2,979
Criminal justice system................		1,685	2,817
Social welfare program administration		142	237
Other (fire losses, fire protection, highway safety)		832	1,391
Indirect:			
Alcoholics incarceration		1,418	2,371
Others' lost worktime due to motor vehicle crashes		354	592
Total Other Related Costs		$ 6,213	$10,387
TOTAL ECONOMIC COSTS		**$49,374**	**$82,553**

SOURCE: Adapted from A.M. Cruze, H.J. Harwood, P.L. Kristiansen, et al., *Economic Costs to Society of Alcohol and Drug Abuse and Mental Illness 1977,* final report prepared by the Research Triangle Insitute for the Alcohol, Drug Abuse, and Mental Health Administration, Department of Health and Human Services, October 1981.

It is important to point out in Table 2 that of the $735 million spent on alcohol support services, such as research, education, training, and insurance administration, only 3.8 percent was spent on research. It follows logically that where there is little research funding, there is little involvement by mainstream medicine and consequently little in the way of treatment innovations or new preventive techniques.

It is evident that the indirect costs of alcohol abuse far exceed the direct costs. Increasing the nation's financial commitment to more and better treatment, research, and prevention will certainly add to direct costs associated with alcohol abuse. However, in the long run, an increase in direct costs may help reduce indirect costs, thus a net savings to the country could still be achieved.

Also, it is clear that the costs associated with treatment are largely consumed by alcohol-induced (or related) illnesses and trauma and *not for the actual treatment of excessive drinking itself.* Of the $5.6 billion expended on treatment, only $707 million (13 percent) can be regarded as money spent for actual alcoholism rehabilitation programs. The remaining $4.9 billion was spent on the medical complications and injuries related to alcohol abuse.

Both analyses by Berry and Cruze reveal that billions of dollars were spent on treating the diseases caused or aggravated by alcohol abuse, such as liver disease and cancer, as well as the alcohol-related injuries. Berry estimated the amount at $12.74 billion in 1975 ($23.19 billion in 1983 dollars), while Cruze et. al. estimated it was $5.6 billion in 1977 ($9.4 billion in 1983 dollars). Even though Berry's estimate was higher than that of Cruze, the National Academy of Science's Institute of Medicine has said that Berry's costs are underestimated.[39]

The Institute of Medicine indicated that Berry's estimate of the health care costs of alcohol abuse were understated by 40 percent, because Berry did not include costs of many alcohol-related problems, such as Fetal Alcohol Syndrome. If Berry had considered these and various other factors, the total economic cost of alcohol abuse would have been $60 billion for 1975, or approach $120 billion in 1983 dollars according to Institute of Medicine researchers.

Despite these alcohol-related health care costs in the billions, comparatively little is spent on treatment and rehabilitation programs for alcoholism treatment per se. Berry et. al. estimated $54 million was spent on alcoholism treatment and rehabilitation. That is approximately one-tenth of one percent of their estimated total economic costs of alcohol misuse and alcoholism to society. Cruze et. al. estimated that $707 million was spent on treating alcoholism and other abuse-specific illnesses in alcohol specialty facilities in 1977. That amount is 1.4 percent of Cruze's estimated total economic costs of alcohol abuse to society.

Another measure of the disparity between the costs to society of the problem and the amount spent on treatment comes from the National Drug and Alcoholism Treatment Utilization Survey which indicated that $1.1 billion was paid for alcoholism treatment in 1982, as reported by 3,997 treatment programs.[40] That amount is still only about one percent of the projected 1983 economic costs of alcohol abuse to society. Under the current system, America spends more money on the consequences of alcohol abuse (e.g., broken bones, cirrhosis, etc.) than it does treating their cause — excessive drinking.

One can sympathize with the reader who, even though the data cited are only a tiny extract from the growing literature, nevertheless feels inundated. The details should not obscure the basic points:

1) Alcoholism is a very costly disease. Yet it is far, far costlier than most of us imagine since few of us appreciate its very substantial impact on productivity.

2) Productivity losses alone are four times the amount expended on treatment costs (including costs of medical care for alcohol-related conditions). When we take account of excess mortality and morbidity, crime, accidents, fire, and similar consequences of alcoholism, we find that collectively these costs are nine times the treatment costs. These ratios increase markedly if we limit treatment costs to alcoholism treatment only.

3) It is no exaggeration to suggest that the state of health of the American economy, as well as that of the society, is severely affected by the presence of alcohol abuse and alcoholism. It is also no exaggeration to suggest that the size of the expenditures on specific treatment of alcoholism (about $1.1 billion) bears little relation to the negative economic and social impacts of the disease.

Clearly, alcohol abuse and its impacts exact a heavy toll in direct and indirect costs. Yet, it is apparent that the cost of treatment (much of it dealing with the consequences of alcohol abuse) is only a small part of the costs of the ailment. The distortion that results if one ignores the indirect costs is clear.

Reductions in alcoholism treatment may reduce dollar expenditures in the very short run. Yet, since treatment is often effective, decreases in treatment of alcoholism will inevitably lead to increases in the costs of treatment of alcohol-related diseases. The presumed short-run savings will disappear. Dollar expenditures will be classified under a different heading, but there will be no reduction in the total. Of even greater significance are the long-run economic impacts, the losses in productivity and income, and the economic losses through crime, automobile accidents, and fire. Furthermore — and the point can not be overstressed since there is more to a society than economics — all these costs have their counterpart in human tragedies.

Thus, the expenditures for treatment of alcoholism and alcohol abuse, though they appear large in an absolute sense, turn out to be relatively small when compared with alcoholism's pervasive impacts and even smaller when we consider that most of the dollars classified as "treatment" are not spent on preventing or curing alcoholism but in treating its associated effects. It is important that those who assess potential health policy measures adopt a broad rather than a narrow definition of health care costs, especially at a time when there is pressure to cut or contain health expenditures. Failing that, they may ignore the equivalent of a raging fire and its potential damage, while focusing on the dollars that might be saved by cutting back expenditures on fire protection and prevention. Faulty accounting and faulty analysis are not likely to lead to sensible policy.

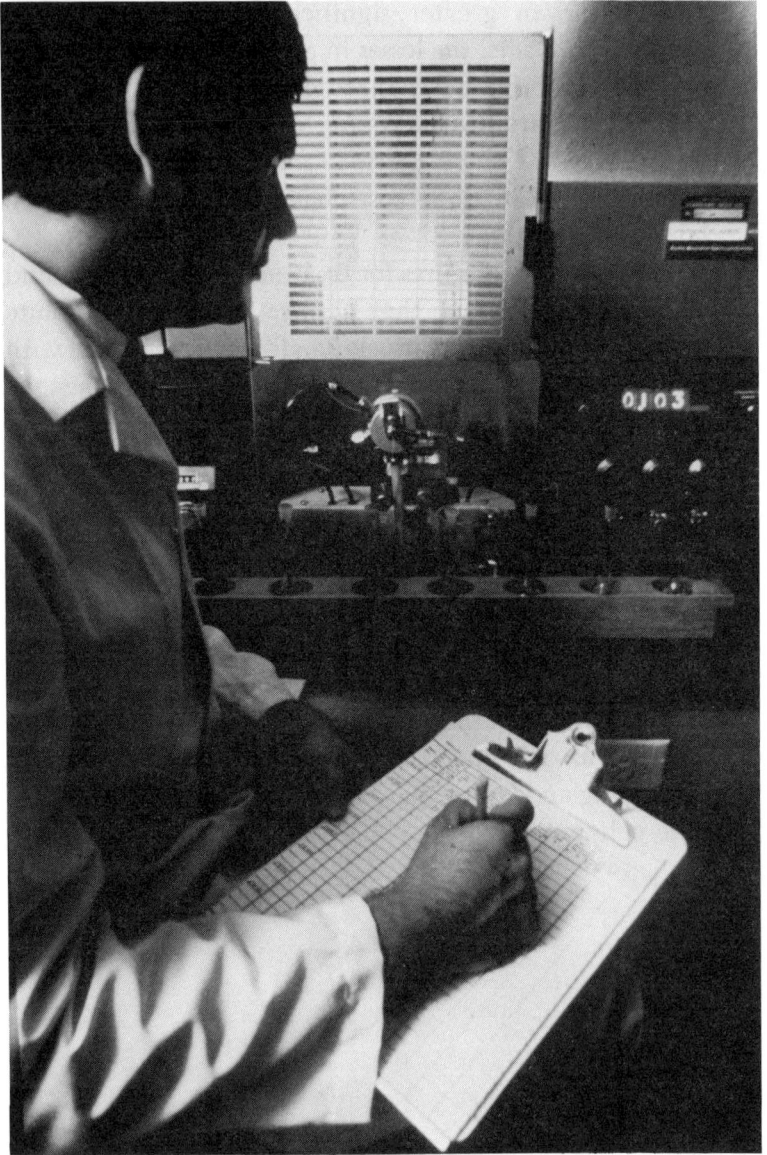

© *William James Warren/WestLight*

4

Alcoholism and Other Diseases
A Comparison of Impact

An additional perspective on alcoholism's importance, on the sums spent as a consequence of its impact, and on the monies expended on treatment, prevention, and research, can be gained by comparing its impacts with those of other major diseases that afflict Americans. Impressive as are the data on indirect costs, we gain perspective from comparative data that provide an additional assessment of the place of alcoholism in the health spectrum. Such comparisons, it should be clear from earlier comments on alcoholism's pervasive impact and on its impact on other diseases and causes of death, are fraught with difficulty. The true significance of alcoholism is likely to be understated, since: (1) the specific causal relationships between alcoholism and various other diseases are not fully understood; (2) in many cases alcoholism is not diagnosed or reported, attention being given to the disease for which the patient sought treatment or for the proximate cause of death.

Cruze et. al. report, "Although the list of illnesses which are found to be caused *totally* (emphasis added) by alcohol abuse is relatively limited, it accounts for a relatively large number of deaths," estimated in 1977, to total 19,000. But the important point is that "there is an extensive list of causes of death for which current research indicates alcohol abuse as either the principal factor involved or at least a secondary factor." Since factors other than alcohol abuse may be involved, only some of the deaths (for diseases with specific data on the proportion due to alcohol abuse) were counted. Even so, of the 97,000 deaths in the category "direct secondary causes," 11,000 were attributed to alcohol abuse. Furthermore, of the 152,000 deaths caused by motor vehicle crashes, falls, fires, homicide, and other accidents, 36,000 were attributable to alcohol abuse. Thus, in 1977, the deaths attributable to alcoholism and alcohol abuse totalled 65,000.[41]

Utilizing the 1980 figures from the National Center for Health Statistics a ranking by disease would show the following death statistics:[42]

1.	Heart disease	761,085
2.	Cancer	416,509
3.	Cerebrovascular diseases	170,225
4.	Alcoholism and alcohol abuse	127,385
5.	Diabetes	34,851

Data on mortality leave no doubt that alcoholism is one of the nation's leading killers. Prevalence data similarly indicate alcoholism's significance. Alcoholism and alcohol abuse are estimated to affect 14.7 million Americans, according to the National Institute on Alcohol Abuse and Alcoholism's percent estimates of alcohol abuse among adults and adolescents. Furthermore, the number of cases of alcoholism increases by an estimated 400,000 cases annually.[43] No one source has estimated the prevalence of major killer diseases in recent years. Thus, there is no valid way to definitely state one disease is more prevalent than another. However, figures compiled by the National Center for Health Statistics, American Cancer Institute, and the National Institute of Alcoholism and Alcohol Abuse indicate the following:[44,45]

	Persons Affected
Heart disease	17,186,000
Alcohol abuse and alcoholism*	14,700,000
Diabetes	5,500,000
Cancer**	5,000,000
Cerebrovascular disease	1,869,000

Again, the fact these figures are drawn from different sources, presumably using different calculation strategies, underscores the need to interpret them with caution. We do know from the Gallup Poll results mentioned earlier that an alarmingly high percentage of Americans regard alcoholism as a major national problem and have experienced problems with it or the abuse of alcohol in their own homes.

One perspective which tends to be lacking in many specialty areas of medicine is an appreciation of how one disease compares with another economically. It is unlikely that many people comparing the costs of diseases would put alcoholism and alcohol abuse at the top of the list. More importantly, legislators, insurers, and treatment providers rarely make economic comparisons between illnesses. While debating cost-benefit proposals, few understand the distinction between direct and indirect costs of a disease.

---

*The alcohol abuse prevalence figure is developed by applying the 1978 percentage of alcoholic and problem drinkers to 1982 population estimates.
**Includes Americans alive today who have a history of cancer but are considered cured.

FIGURE 1

COMPARATIVE COSTS OF ILLNESSES

Cost in Billions $

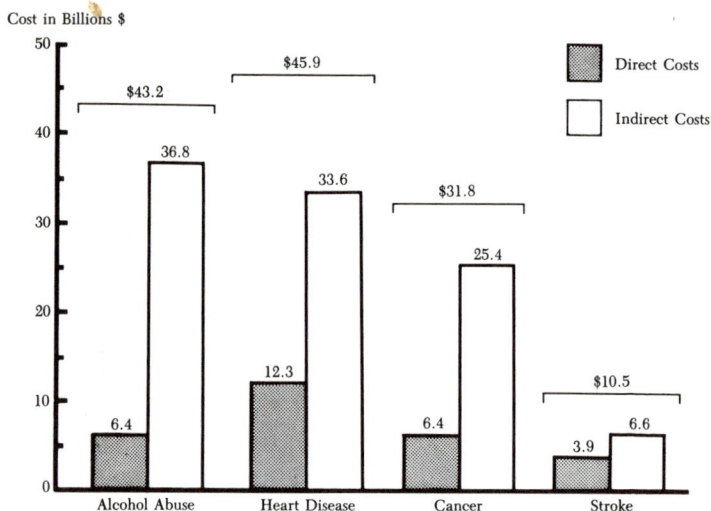

*National Center for Health Statistics, *"Tables, and Charts for Sex Differences in Mortality and Morbidity: Some Aspects of the Economic Burden."* Prepared by Dorothy P. Rice, Dec. 4, 1981.

Figure 1 depicts the direct and indirect costs of alcohol abuse, heart disease, cancer, and stroke.[46] It shows that the total economic costs to society associated with alcohol abuse/alcoholism are nearly equal to heart disease, this nation's most prevalent killer disease. And the economic costs of alcohol abuse are 4 times greater than those of strokes and 1.4 times greater than those of cancer. Thus, despite being frequently overlooked in the ordering of public health expenditure priorities, alcohol abuse/alcoholism is one of our nation's most costly health problems.

Even though heart disease and alcohol abuse cost this nation nearly the same, almost twice as much is spent on treating heart disease as is spent on treating alcoholism and alcohol-related medical conditions. Although indirect costs exceed direct costs in each of these diseases, the discrepancy is far greater in the case of alcohol abuse than for other diseases. As indicated in Figure 1 the indirect costs of alcohol abuse are 5.8 times greater than its direct costs, while the comparable ratios for other illnesses are 4.0 to 1 for cancer, 2.7 to 1 for heart disease and 1.7 to 1 for strokes.

Costs of treating alcoholism are relatively low compared to the costs of treating some other life-threatening illnesses. A 20 percent sample of how much Medicare paid out for patients treated in acute-care hospitals during calendar year of 1981, organized by diagnosis, illustrates this disparity.[47]

Diagnosis Related Group	*Description*	*Average Charge Per Case—1981*
DRG 14	Specific cerebrovascular disorders except TIA	$ 4,480
DRG 107	Coronary bypass	$15,676
DRG 129	Cardiac arrest	$ 5,357
DRG 294	Diabetes in patients thirty-six years of age or older	$ 2,661
DRG 436	Alcohol dependence	$ 2,802

The disparities also exist in research funding. Comparing the amount of federal dollars spent on research for major disease, researchers found significant differences.[48]

$ in millions (1981)[49]	
Cancer	$772
Heart and vascular disease	$327
Respiratory disease	$ 80
Alcoholism and abuse	$ 22

The amount spent on cancer research is 35 times that spent on alcoholism and abuse, the amount spent on heart and vascular disease is 15 times; and respiratory disease is nearly 4 times.

In conclusion, alcoholism is far more prevalent than is commonly believed. However, most Americans are likely unaware that it is among the top four most common chronic conditions or that, even under conservative assumptions, it ranks as one of the leading causes of death!

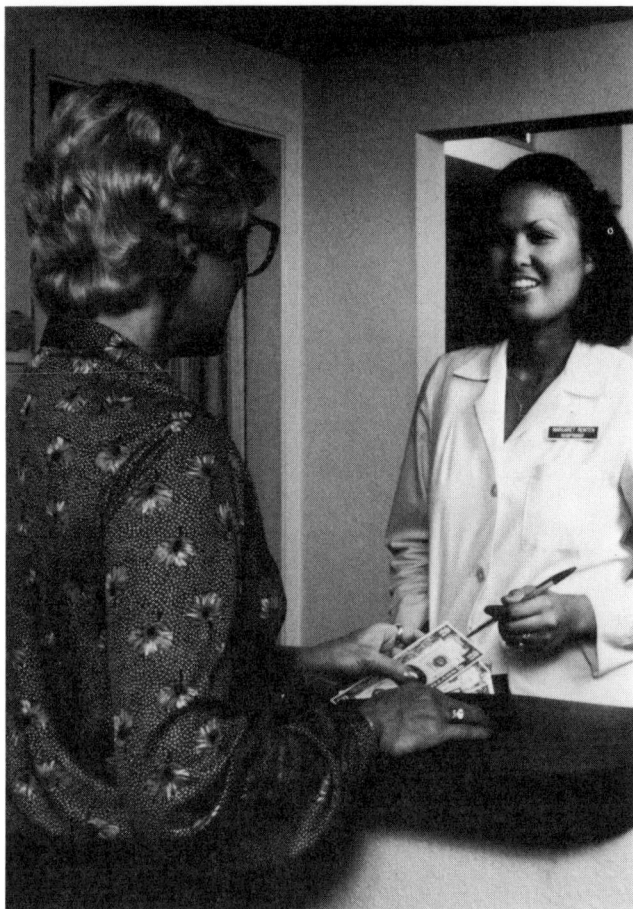

© *Campbell & Boulanger/WestLight*

5

The Cost of Treating Alcoholism
An Investment in America

Alcoholism and alcohol abuse are pervasive national health problems. Unfortunately, much less is spent on research, prevention, and treatment than is warranted. This often happens in health care spending as a result of a distorted perspective, i.e., when the indirect costs of a disease and thus the investment component of health expenditures are ignored. These indirect costs and the potential return on investment are especially important in the case of alcoholism because of its attendant impacts on mortality, morbidity, and productivity as well as on crime, accidents, and fire.

That alcoholism treatment in fact is underfunded is, of course, not *proven* by the statement of *theoretical* reasons why underfunding might occur or by the observation that alcoholism is a costly disease. The impact of alcoholism must be compared to actual treatment costs, to the probability of successful treatment, and to institutional reimbursement and financing mechanisms as they exist in the health and medical care industry. In this chapter some of these matters will be discussed, giving special emphasis to the total costs of alcoholism treatment and the sources of payment and reimbursement. The reader is cautioned that the data on the costs of treatment are limited to specific treatment for alcoholism. They do *not* include costs of treating other illnesses which are affected or influenced by alcoholism and therefore are not comparable to the data already cited. Conversely, however, they are far more descriptive of the sums being spent to *cure* alcoholism. Thus, they can be considered as approximating the investment component of alcoholism treatment and can be contrasted with the economic impact of alcoholism, including the consequent increases in total health expenditures.

As indicated earlier Cruze estimated that $5.6 billion was spent in 1977 projected at $9.4 billion in 1983 — for the treatment of alcohol-connected illnesses and injuries. Thus, these sums are not limited to the treatment of alcohol abuse per se. The total funding for alcoholism treatment is, of course, much less. The 1982 National Drug and Alcoholism Treatment Utilization Survey (NDATUS) reports that the nation's alcoholism treatment units received a total of $1.1 billion in 1982,[50] which accounts for 0.3 percent of the National Health Expenditures totaling $322 billion.[51] From 1980 to 1982, funding for alcoholism increased by 19.4 percent from $940.5 million to $1.1 billion.[52] In contrast, funding for national health care increased by 30.4 percent from $249 billion to $322 billion.[53]

The 3,997 alcoholism units reporting financial information in the 1982 NDATUS survey received their funds — as do all parts of the health sector — from multiple sources. The largest single source was private health insurance, which accounted for $296.4 million, or 26 percent of the $1.1 billion. This is a comparatively *low* percentage. In 1982, for example, private health insurance accounted for 26.6 percent of total expenditures for dentists' services, for 35.1 percent of physicians' services and 33.1 percent for hospital care. It, of course, is true that other third-party payments plus federal, state, and local government payment and support — via appropriations rather than insurance — are available for alcoholism treatment. As a consequence, patient-direct payment provided only about 10 percent of the funding for alcohol treatment (as contrasted with 68.7 percent for dentistry, 37.4 percent for physicians' services and 12.1 percent for hospital care).[54,55]

The fact that a low percentage of expenditures is accounted for by patient-direct payment or private health insurance, however, serves to emphasize the vulnerability of alcoholism treatment centers and programs to shifting government and philanthropic priorities in an era of constrained budgets. The fact cannot be overstressed that, unlike the rest of health care, alcoholism treatment is highly dependent on non-insurance government funding:[56]

- State governments provide 21 percent of total funds.

- Local governments provide an additional 10 percent.

- Federal government accounts for 15 percent, including 4 percent under the Alcohol, Drug Abuse and Mental Health Administration's block grant program.

- Third parties provide 40 percent (26 percent, private health insurance; 7 percent, public health insurance; and an additional 7 percent through state and local fees for service, public welfare, social services block grants.

- An additional 14 percent comes from client fees and other sources.

Alcoholism Treatment Funding
By Source

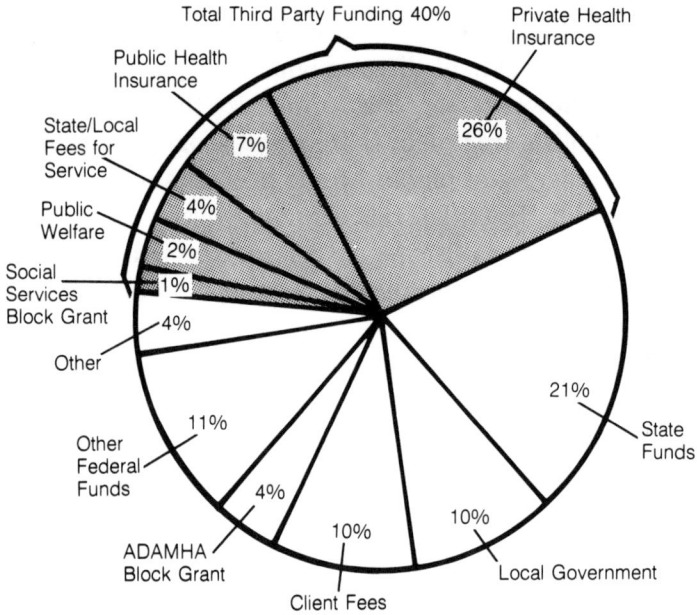

Total Third Party Funding 40%

Private Health Insurance

Public Health Insurance — 7%

State/Local Fees for Service — 4%

Public Welfare — 2%

Social Services Block Grant — 1%

Other — 4%

Other Federal Funds — 11%

ADAMHA Block Grant — 4%

Client Fees — 10%

Local Government — 10%

State Funds — 21%

26%

Total Reported Funding: $1,123,175,000
(3997 Units)

Source: NDATUS, September 30, 1982

The variability and instability in funding is illustrated by comparing 1980 and 1982 data from the National Drug and Alcoholism Treatment Utilization Surveys. In that time period total treatment center funding grew from $940.5 million to $1.1 billion, an increase of 19.4 percent. Yet, from 1980 to 1982, federal funding for treatment increased by only 1.5 percent. From 1979 to 1980, federal funding had increased by 10 percent. State government funding between 1980 and 1982 increased by 14.4 percent, but between 1979 to 1980 it increased by only 1.6 percent. Other variations are also noticeable. From 1980 to 1982 funding for New York treatment programs grew by 15 percent, whereas funding for California programs grew by 27 percent.[57] During that same time period, funding for programs under public ownership grew by only 12.7 percent, while funding for privately owned programs grew by 28.9 percent.

The preceding data illuminate a number of funding characteristics:

- The fact that sources of funding vary significantly from year to year leads to instability in operation and type of clientele. It is extremely difficult to engage in rational planning or to capture gains in economic efficiency under such circumstances.

- A high proportion of funds are received from government at all levels. These funds become available via public insurance as well as via programs that operate through the appropriation process. The latter do not contribute to stability. Furthermore, even federal third-party funding (including, for example, Medicare and Medicaid) is also at risk as the general atmosphere of belt-tightening for social programs leads to changes in program support, regulations, and reimbursement policies.

Alcoholism programs have never been well supported relative to the dimensions of the problem, as measured by the loss in production, by the small percentage of the affected population who are in treatment programs, or by the medical care costs of associated diseases. Today, these alcoholism programs are especially vulnerable and at risk. The sources of payment for treatment are largely the different levels of government. At a time of tight social budgets and shifting priorities, in an atmosphere in which the presumption is that medical expenditures are not only high but excessive, one cannot assume that the support for alcohol treatment programs will increase in real terms sufficient to meet real needs. Indeed, those concerned with alcohol treatment programs will find it necessary to fight hard to maintain the real level of government spending and effort now available.

© Pierre Kopp/WestLight

6

Alcoholism
The Insurance Factor

Earlier the various factors that could lead to underspending on treatment of alcoholism were discussed. Many of these related to attitudes and behavior of patients and individuals at risk. Others related to attitudes and priorities of deliverers of care. In addition, there is a problem resulting from the fact that the data used in discussing the costs of illness focus on actual expenditures and do not include indirect costs.

Also discussed were the various sources of payment for and expenditures on alcoholism treatment, noting the relatively small role played by private health insurance and the large role played by government funding. It was indicated that present funding patterns lend themselves to potential instability.

Given the importance of alcoholism and given the importance of third-party reimbursement in funding care and treatment in the rest of the health sector, one must consider why private health insurance plays such a small role in the case of alcoholism. In looking to the future, one must ask whether third-party coverage for alcoholism treatment can be expanded, in spite of the general pressures for cutbacks in benefits and for cost containment.

Clearly, the future of alcoholism treatment depends critically on the linkages developed between treatment and public and private insurance programs, that is, with third-party payment mechanisms.

Third-party payment has as one of its purposes the minimizing of the monetary barrier to care (usually defined as the direct costs of medical care and not including the loss of wages and salaries, transportation, and time). The role of insurance in payment for care, and thus in removing the barrier to care and treatment, has been shown to be significant in encouraging the use of care. Conversely, the absence of insurance coverage reduces treatment among those who need help, especially in the case of expensive procedures or in the case of chronic as contrasted with acute conditions. Lack of third-party payment will likely also lead to postponement or delay of treatment, a situation that would be especially unfortunate in the case of alcoholism. Consequently, it is clear that insurance coverage has a considerable impact on the number of patients treated and expenditures on treatment.

Our review of the relationship between alcoholism and insurance will be limited to health insurance. Yet it is worth noting that there is a relationship to the life insurance industry. This was pointed out as early as the latter part of the nineteenth century. In discussing the influence of alcohol on mortality and on life insurance premiums, Henry W. Blair, United States senator from New Hampshire, concluded that if the excess mortality due to alcoholism were eliminated because everyone was abstinent, life insurance premiums could be reduced by 40 percent.[58] While the specific estimate is certainly different today, the point made remains of interest, especially since a significant proportion of health insurance is sold by companies that also sell life insurance.

To begin with, of all alcoholics 85 percent do not receive treatment. There are many reasons for this high percentage:[59]

- The denial syndrome often prevents the individual from recognizing that he or she has a problem with alcohol. Dr. Paul Ohliger explained denial is not the result of dishonesty so much as the result of delusional thinking of alcoholism. The delusions result from chemically induced blackouts wherein the brain apparently fails to make a "memory tape." The toxic effects of alcohol on the brain produce psychological blackouts wherein the brain refuses to recall painful events and euphorically recalls past painful events as being pleasant.

- Significant others are unable to help the alcoholic because they don't know how to approach someone who doesn't want help.

- There is a lack of awareness of treatment resources.

- Confidentiality is a concern.

- Stigma and shame surrounding alcoholism discourage many from seeking treatment.

These factors which decrease the number of people who seek treatment are exacerbated by the fact that until relatively recently, insurance coverage for the treatment of alcoholism was also limited. Poor insurance was due, in part, to the view that alcoholism was a self-inflicted disease, raising the issue of moral hazard and calling into question whether insurance was an appropriate vehicle for community sharing of risks and costs.

The absence of insurance and third-party payment was also explained by the fact that insurers believed that inclusion of alcoholism benefits would necessitate large increases in premiums as a consequence of the large number of people who might need treatment, high utilization of services by patients, and weak cost control on providers. They were especially concerned that, given the prevalence of alcoholism, there would be a "catch-up" effect leading to extremely high costs in the first few years. Nevertheless, the barriers to the inclusion of alcoholism treatment did begin to fall in the early 1970s as a consequence of the general expansion of insurance coverage of non-hospital and outpatient treatment and in response to specific pressures for coverage of alcoholism. Blue Cross/Blue Shield and a number of commercial insurance carriers removed their standard exclusion of alcoholism treatment and state legislatures took a greater interest in defining benefit packages. As of 1982, the fifty states fell into three distinct categories in regard to alcoholism treatment insurance: twenty made alcoholism coverage mandatory for most health insurance policies (it should, however, be remembered that not everyone has health insurance coverage); fifteen required that group insurers provide alcoholism coverage as an option; fifteen placed no requirements.[60,61]

Experience shows, as insurance coverage expands, that many of the earlier fears of insurers were unfounded. The use of treatment services has not been excessive. In fact, given the prevalence of alcoholism, it is reasonable to conclude that treatment has been underutilized (either because demand for care has not been as great as was hypothesized or because the limited supply of treatment facilities and programs could not be increased rapidly). Preliminary studies indicate that when the insurance benefit is added, utilization of treatment services increases — as, of course, is desirable. The increases, however, are not overwhelming and are far below the generally accepted prevalence rate for alcoholism. On the basis of a number of studies of alcoholism insurance programs, Blue Cross and Blue Shield conclude that "utilization is low, usually less than three-tenths of one percent of the covered population."[62]

Nevertheless, the expansion of private coverage for alcoholism treatment has been limited. Results of the 1981 "Level of Benefits Study" by the Bureau of Labor Statistics were analyzed by Krizay and Carels. Using 1981 figures, this study indicated that only 38 percent of full-time private sector employees in eight major industries have any coverage for alcohol abuse treatment. While 62 percent of employees in mining had some coverage, the figure dropped to 24 percent of those employed in service industries. The 38 percent contrasted sharply with the data for various optional procedures: 10 percent for diagnostic X-ray and laboratory, 97 percent for prescription drugs, and 61 percent for dental care. Furthermore, only half of those who had alcoholism treatment coverage were covered for outpatient treatment by mental health specialists, thus indicating the very limited extent of coverage even for those who have any coverage at all.[63]

It would be fallacious to argue that insurance companies have offered alcoholism treatment benefits, but that, given the level of premiums, subscribers have opted not to buy the benefits. As we shall see, premiums for alcoholism benefits can be quite modest, so modest, in fact, that one cannot help but conclude that a major factor explaining the low level of private insurance is the less than aggressive marketing of alcoholism benefits on the part of many insurers. This is the case despite the fact that alcoholism treatment has been found to be effective. The U.S. Office of Technology Assessment, after conducting an extensive study into the effectiveness of alcoholism treatment concluded that *any treatment of alcoholism is better than no treatment.*[64] Average success rates calculated for various studies indicate that about two-thirds of those treated improve. Treatment for alcoholism results in subsequent reductions in treatment for other health disorders. Thus, the lack of alcoholism insurance coverage would markedly increase associated health care costs. Put simply, the failure to spend a dollar on "A" increases the need to spend dollars on "B."

A 1980 study by Zook and Moore found that a comparatively small fraction of hospital patients, about 13 percent, utilized more than half of the hospital resources in a year.[65] Most of these high-cost patients were suffering from alcoholism. They also smoked too much and were overweight. In a follow-up study, Zook, Savickis, and Moore noted that the typical high-cost patient experienced multiple hospitalizations for the same disease.[66] Patients with a history of chronic alcoholism had a much higher incidence of repeated hospitalizations than individuals with no alcoholism noted in their histories. The authors noted that public health policies targeted at these high-cost "repeater" patients might well achieve major economies. They cited the example of a follow-up program for diabetics which reduced the incidence of hospital readmissions in that group by 56 percent.

Certainly, studies on alcoholism treatment have shown substantial reductions in medical utilization following treatment. A 1979 literature review reports that alcoholism treatment is linked to declines in sick days between 38 to 47 percent, in medical utilization between 26 and 60 percent, in dollars paid in sickness and accident benefits of between 33 and 48 percent. Thus, the costs of alcoholism insurance and treatment may be offset by reduced expenditures elsewhere in the health care system.[67]

The National Institute for Alcohol Abuse and Alcoholism has published a study which examines the cost implications of six model insurance benefit packages.[68] These involve different insurance packages and insurer configurations (fee-for-service or prepayment). The various models are associated with substantial differences in benefits paid over a five-year period (more limited plans, as might be expected, are used less). Importantly, the study develops "alcoholism treatment offset estimates" which are defined as "savings (the reduction in costs for total health care resulting from misdiagnosis as well as the result of untreated alcoholism) associated with coverage of alcoholism treatment."

In four of the six cases (plans that provide more extensive coverage) the savings *exceed* the cost of the benefits paid. The report concludes that in 1981 dollars, the monthly initial premium increase (before the benefits of the offsets are realized) would have ranged between 14 cents and $1.15. Even these relatively modest premium increases are reduced when account is taken of the offset savings in other costs. Then the monthly health insurance premium costs decrease: the monthly costs for two models which still involve positive costs drop from $0.14 to $0.06 and from $0.34 to $0.16. For the other prototypes, *involving "richer" benefit packages*, the monthly premiums now become negative (that is, the reduction in premiums associated with other health care costs exceeds the cost of treatment benefits). Monthly savings range between $0.04 to $0.52. Alcohol insurance more than pays for itself (even with a narrow definition which focuses on direct rather than indirect costs and benefits). The study makes it clear that the treatment of alcoholism, given its secondary effects, is a good buy: total health insurance premiums can decrease if alcoholism benefits are added to the insurance package.

Regrettably, that is not enough to assure that alcoholism insurance will grow, given the skepticism that spending money in the health field will save money in the long run and given the way our health care system is financed. The money spent on alcoholism treatment might, for example, come from one pocket, the savings and monetary benefits might accrue to others. Given a national perspective, it would make economic sense for the nation or even the single employer to "invest" in alcoholism treatment. America's health care expenditures, however, are financed from multiple sources, each with its own "bottom-line" requirements. Individual employers or employees may conclude that what makes economic sense for the nation does not make sense for them. It is possible that the individual employer would not capture all the benefits of lower absenteeism or higher productivity. Similarly, the individual employee might find that he or she is asked to bear the costs of alcoholism treatment (or premiums) while the costs of treatment of the health conditions caused or contributed to by alcoholism are borne by the employer. There are many situations in which one party might pay for the costs of treatment while other parties reap the economic benefits.

Education may help in overcoming skepticism. Americans, after all, do understand the nature of investment. It is difficult to believe that public discussion of the benefits of alcohol treatment and of the role of insurance would not make a substantial difference. The second problem related to multiple payers can also be solved. In situations with those characteristics, the mandating of insurance coverage is a solution. Such insurance should cover all members of society. Short of that universal approach, which involves basic social issues that extend beyond the question of benefits for alcoholism treatment, one could mandate the addition of an alcoholism treatment benefit in those private and public insurance programs in existence (and any new ones undertaken).

Such an approach would not resolve the issue of alcohol insurance for those without any health insurance. It would, nevertheless, assure that those who do have insurance coverage would have alcoholism benefits. The extension of alcoholism benefits need not wait for the resolution of the next "great" debate on the way health care is financed in the United States. Indeed, it can be argued that major government insurance plans (e.g., Medicare) have tended to build on the patterns that already exist in the private market. They may well be the case in the future as well. It is, therefore, doubly important to extend private insurance for alcoholism treatment further. Failing that, alcoholism benefits may be neglected in future government initiatives.

In December 1983, the President's Commission on Drunk Driving made the following recommendations:[69]

- Rehabilitation and education programs for individuals convicted of driving under the influence should be provided as a supplement to other sanctions, and not as a replacement for those sanctions.

- Pre-sentence investigations, including alcohol assessments conducted by qualified personnel, should be available to all courts in order to appropriately classify the defendant's problem with alcohol. Repeat offenders should be required to undergo medical screening for alcoholism by a physician trained in alcoholism, an alcoholism counselor, or by an approved treatment facility.

- Alcohol education programs should be used only for those first offenders who are classified as social drinkers and for those who have had no previous exposure to alcohol education programs. Problem drinkers and repeat offenders should be referred to more intensive rehabilitation programs.

- Alcohol treatment and rehabilitation programs should be available for individuals judged to need such services. The programs should be tailored to the individual's needs, and the individual should be assigned to such programs for a length of time determined by treatment personnel and enforced by court probation.

- State insurance commissioners should require and/or state legislators should enact legislation requiring health insurance providers to include coverage for the treatment and rehabilitation of alcohol and other drug dependent persons in all health insurance policies.

The Commission concluded that education or treatment be exercised as a carefully chosen response to the offender's particular problem with alcohol. They recognized that alcoholism is an illness and should be covered by health insurance programs. Without such coverage, individuals tend to ignore treatment. Lastly, according to the Commission, "In the long run, insurance carriers and society end up paying more if coverage is not provided."

It should be clear that mandating of benefits would not solve a number of the problems associated with alcoholism treatment. In addition to the philosophic or ideologic objections that some individuals and groups may raise against mandating, there is the pragmatic issue: the availability of benefits does not assure their utilization. Data on increased utilization, in fact, suggest that utilization does increase, but not greatly. That can be taken as an indication of the pervasive impact of the way that society, employers, potential patients, and the medical community view alcoholism. It can also be taken as an indication of the educational task still required and of the importance of outreach efforts. Our concern should be with treatment, and we delude ourselves if we fail to recognize that the lack of insurance is only one of a number of factors reducing the care and treatment of alcoholism.

An additional issue concerns the nature of the treatment benefits to be covered. Clearly, the benefits should be related to appropriate treatment modalities and settings.

Nevertheless, we cannot assume that this will be the case. Cost containment efforts are likely to lead the pressures to restrict in-hospital care on the presumption that out-of-hospital services are less expensive (there may also be pressure to restrict outpatient after-care for individuals who have been hospitalized). While economists are not in a position to judge which particular treatment is most effective for a particular patient, experience with various reimbursement mechanisms and insurance programs, as well as with the nature of our health care system and its financing, does permit the following general observations.

A shift from inpatient to outpatient treatment may be appropriate for some patients, but quite inappropriate for others. While follow-ups on individuals who have been treated in inpatient or outpatient programs show that outcomes are fairly similar, researchers have found that those entering inpatient programs are generally sicker. They have more signs of dependence on alcohol, are more likely to be depressed, generally consume more alcohol than the outpatients prior to admission, and experience more social alienation and withdrawal.[70,71]

Restriction of benefits, however, is likely to influence the clinical decision and, as a consequence, may negate any potential cost reductions. If, for example, only outpatient care is covered, it is predictable that some, perhaps many, patients will be shunted to that form of treatment. Money isn't saved when less is spent if that is accompanied by a reduction of the effectiveness of treatment. The goal ought to be to get value for money, not to spend as few dollars as possible. In this regard, it is instructive to note that the cost simulation study already mentioned found that prepaid plans with every incentive to reduce inpatient care by substituting outpatient care, in fact had about the same admissions rate to inpatient care and had a *longer* length of stay than fee-for-service modalities.

It is not at all clear that restriction of inpatient benefits would, in fact, save dollars. There are at last three additional problems. The first relates to the systems of review, monitoring, control, and quality assessment for outpatient treatment that would be necessary. Without such systems there is a risk of rapid escalation of unwarranted and/or ineffective outpatient care. Of course, it is important to adopt the most cost-effective treatment. It is, however, true that in the real world that which may appear cost-effective on a per case basis may be less so when extended to a total population.

The second problem relates to the fact that if acute care for most illnesses is covered but in-hospital care for alcoholism is not, some of the presumed gains will disappear as patients continue to be admitted to acute-care facilities under surrogate diagnoses. Again, money isn't saved by simply reclassifying the expenditures. Nor is this solely a problem of "misclassification." Some patients will require hospitalization for conditions associated with alcoholism. It would be costly if they could not receive hospital care that addressed the full range of problems, but, instead, had to be treated in different settings and at different times for their interrelated conditions.

The American health sector has had experience with the influence of in-hospital and out-of-hospital coverage for certain conditions, but not for others. The experience suggests that insurance coverage does affect clinical care decisions and disease classification. It also argues that insurance restrictions are a poor and cumbersome substitute for provider and patient education and especially so in a heterogeneous population needing various modalities of treatment.

Finally, we must ask what would happen to hospital beds if benefits for inpatient care for alcoholism were excluded. If those beds remained empty but in service, hospital cost savings would be minimal. The cost of an empty bed is not insignificant. It is quite possible that rates for the full beds would have to rise in order to support the empty bed. Nor would the system save dollars if the bed, given its availability and the incentive to fill it, were occupied by a patient who stayed in the hospital longer or who didn't need hospitalization. Unless unneeded beds — or more correctly, unneeded wings or hospitals — were closed down, presumed savings would be far different than would be projected from a simple (and fallacious) comparison of in-hospital and out-of-hospital treatment (even assuming equal effectiveness). Indeed, if hospitals have excess capacity and if ambulatory care would require capital expenditures to expand their services, the "savings" might well become additional costs.

It should be clear that this is not to be taken as an argument for a costly modality of care in preference to one less costly. Rather, it is an argument whose premise is that no single modality of treatment is appropriate for all alcoholics, and whose thesis is that even though one form of care is inherently less expensive on a per-case basis, it should not simply be assumed that these savings can be captured without other changes in the health care system and its financing mechanisms.

All of us should be diligent in searching for economies, but all of us should recognize that to attain such economies will require more than a "nibbling at the edges" or arbitrary restriction of benefits. Given the substantial impact that the structure of coverage can have, the lack of certainty about appropriate care, the heterogeneity of alcoholism patients, the association of alcoholism with other acute and chronic conditions, and the complexity of health care financing, it appears premature, at best, to presume that the insurance system should be used to deny benefits for particular forms of care or that doing so would yield real savings.

It should also be clear that a number of the general trends in the health economy and in health insurance — even aside from the budget constraints already discussed — do not bode well for alcoholism treatment. The characteristics of alcoholism (including the denial by many individuals that they suffer from the disease), for example, suggest there is a very real risk in the new "competitive" approach, which has found favor with some analysts and legislators. This approach stresses price competition and multiple insurance options laid out cafeteria style from which people are free to choose. In this arena, who will choose coverage for herpes, AIDS, or alcoholism? Given the nature of alcoholism, it is reasonable to conclude that unless alcoholism treatment benefits are mandated in all options, it is likely that many individuals will undervalue and not elect to purchase alcoholism treatment coverage. This may be especially true if the number of options were limited (say, a high and low at the extreme). In that case, the low option would be offered at a much lower premium reflecting the limited number of benefits. Since individuals would not be able to select the low option and add selected benefits (including alcoholism treatment), those who are most price sensitive or who believe they are less at risk would likely be left without alcoholism treatment benefits.

Nor is it at all clear that insurance companies would be able to calculate the actuarial costs of including alcoholism treatment under "competition," since with multiple options available to the individual, there will be a much greater problem of self-selection. Indeed, if one views the timing of alcoholism treatment as elective, there is the additional risk that individuals would select the low option, shifting to the high one at the time that they decide to get treatment. The problem of self-selection would be especially severe because, though alcoholism has acute manifestations, it also has chronic characteristics.

In considering the extension of alcoholism treatment, we have to consider the effectiveness of treatment and the potential benefits that can be realized from effective intervention. We must remember to take as wide a view of the benefits as the data permit since alcohol treatment may reduce other health care costs as a consequence of health improvement. The measurement problem is especially complex since with the availability of alcoholism treatment benefits, some treatments, now classified under other diagnoses in order to obtain reimbursement ("surrogate" diagnoses) will be correctly attributed to alcoholism itself. Given the data issues, there is all the more reason for a broad and comprehensive perspective.

Alcoholism is expensive and can be treated. Recovery rates are high. But it should be noted that alcoholism is not a disease that is simply "out there" and exogenous to the individual's behavior. In spite of our ignorance about many of the factors that predispose or lead to alcoholism, there is much that is known. Among the things we do know are that, at present, efforts at treatment and especially at prevention are offset to a significant degree by efforts to promote the use of alcohol and to increase the number of individuals who drink it.

The issue of the promotion of the use of alcohol is not raised in order to suggest restricting behavior by banning alcohol. Prohibition can be opposed on philosophic and/or pragmatic grounds. Rather, it is raised in order to point out the fact that treatment costs are modest in relation to promotion costs: expenditures on advertising of alcoholic beverages exceeded $1 billion in 1981 (up 1 percent over 1980), an amount approximately equal to the sums spent for treatment.[72] The largest share, 44 percent, went to television with an additional 1 percent to radio (in spite of the fact that these include only beer and wine advertising). This advertising, much of it directed at the broad public, is approximately four times greater than government expenditures for alcohol abuse, education, and training.

Clearly, alcohol advertising is not designed to promote alcohol abuse. It is equally clear, however, that alcohol advertising, unless we assume it is designed only to change market shares, expands the total market. While we have no data on the degree to which the encouragement of consumption increases the number who abuse alcohol (perhaps those who become abusers do not need advertising to introduce them to alcohol or to stimulate consumption), one cannot help but be troubled by a situation in which more is spent on advertising alcohol than is spent on treatment or on programs to acquaint individuals with its dangers. The controversy about whether the nation can afford to fund more prevention and treatment efforts, and whether to broaden or cut back on insurance, seems especially ironic when we consider how many resources are devoted to alcohol promotion.

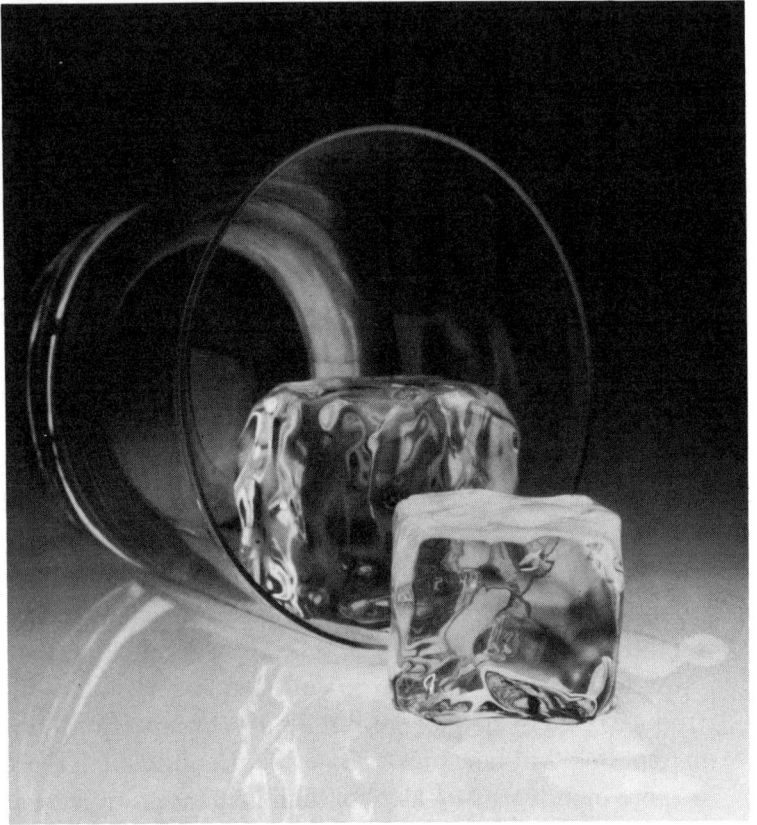

© *Roger Allyn Lee/After-Image*

7

Alcoholism in America
The Price We Pay

The problem of alcoholism cannot be wished away. Its impacts and costs are real and we all bear them. Our review of the various issues and of earlier studies leads us to the following conclusions:

- The economic as well as human costs of alcoholism are very large. There is evidence that, in relation to these costs, America is spending far too little on alcoholism treatment, research, and prevention.

- This underspending is, in part, a symptom of a basic set of attitudes toward alcoholism, attitudes that can be found in virtually all sectors of the society. Alcoholism is a disease but one toward which the medical community, potential patients, the general public, and third-party payers have complex and ambivalent reactions.

- Alcoholism treatment faces the traditional financing problem that plagues other chronic conditions whose prevalence is high and whose treatment is complex, in part because it involves social supports and psychological dimensions. Third-party payers are more comfortable with a purely medical model.

• Alcoholism faces an additional problem created by the failure to take adequate account of many of the associated indirect costs of the disease.

• The extension of alcoholism treatment insurance is subject to attacks by those who share a moralistic perspective which, in its most benign form, says: "Why should I pay to take care of the problem that you have because of the lifestyle you've chosen?" Others share a cynical view toward the health professions, arguing that providers are self-serving maximizers of profit and their recommendations, therefore, are self-serving and suspect.

• Alcoholism treatment insurance faces a situation not of its own making: cost containment. This has resulted in pressures to reduce rather than to expand coverage. The fact that alcoholism treatment reaches only 15 percent of the population that needs help suggests that strong outreach programs are required to expand utilization. Nevertheless, alcoholism treatment insurance is caught in the cost-saving mood and in policies designed to reduce utilization of services.

Given the costs of alcoholism and the relatively small efforts to deal with the problem, a problem exacerbated by the fact that many Americans are conditioned to believe that drinking alcohol is a sign of maturity, sophistication, and sexuality, there is a need for more direct public and private policies specifically targeted on alcoholism and for additional biomedical and social research:

- Additional and more effective informational and educational efforts are needed, aimed at employers, employees and third-party payers. Such efforts should include information on risk elements, on the true costs of alcoholism and its pervasive impacts, on the effectiveness of treatment and its costs. Attention should be given to the large efforts now devoted to alcohol promotion and to the need to offset those efforts.

- It is necessary to continue efforts to broaden third-party coverage for alcoholism prevention and treatment efforts. In furthering this objective, it will be useful to develop appropriate reimbursement techniques and cost containment efforts. Particular emphasis should be placed on more refined criteria for categorizing problem drinking, alcohol abuse and alcoholism and on gaining increased understanding of the efficacy of treatment of these various conditions. Such efforts will be more useful than arbitrary restriction of insurance benefits.

- Public and private policy will continue to develop in an evolutionary fashion and in response to the contributions of the research community. The amount spent and the effort directed at research on alcohol is far less than the costs of the disease warrant. Increased

research on the natural history of the disease,
on risk elements, on social components of
alcoholism, on barriers to treatment, as well
as patterns of treatment are required.

Of overriding importance is the need to remind those
who allocate funds and who make or influence policy that
macro actions designed to contain the level of total health
expenditures and health care inflation will not hit all
diseases and conditions with equal impact or in an appropriate manner. Alcoholism treatment is under-funded
at the present time. It — and the people affected by it —
should not be held liable or share a disproportionate burden
for the financial ills that beset the American health sector.

Alcoholism treatment is an excellent "investment." Even
the narrowest economic accounting indicates that it more
than pays for itself in reductions of other health care costs.
If one considers the impact that alcoholism has on productivity, the "investment" becomes even more beneficial.
When, in addition, account is taken of the human and
social impacts of alcoholism, one is forced to conclude that
the failure to address the problem and to expand treatment
is a measure of our social irresponsibility.

References

1. American Hospital Association, *Who Cares About an Alcoholism Program in the General Hospital* (Chicago: American Hospital Association, 1972), p. 9.

2. National Institute on Alcohol Abuse and Alcoholism, *Third Special Report to the U.S. Congress on Alcohol and Health* (Rockville, Md.: National Institute on Alcohol Abuse and Alcoholism, Alcohol, Drug Abuse and Mental Health Administration, June, 1978), p. 74.

3. *Monday Morning Report*, May 24, 1982, p.2.

4. Irving J. Lewis and Cecil G. Sheps, *The Sick Citadel: The American Academic Medical Center and the Public Interest* (Cambridge, Mass.: Oelgeschlager, Gunn and Hain, 1983), p. 141.

5. The Gallup Organization, *Alcohol Abuse in America* (Princeton, N.J.: November, 1982).

6. Office of Technology Assessment, *Health Technology Case Study 22: The Effectiveness and Costs of Alcoholism Treatment* (Washington, D.C.: Congress of the United States, Office of Technology Assessment, March, 1983), pp. 9, 19.

7. Office of the Assistant Secretary for Health and Surgeon General, *Healthy People — The Surgeon General's Report on Health Promotion and Disease Prevention* (Washington, D.C.: U.S. Department of Health, Education and Welfare, 1979), p. 125.

8. William Mayer, testimony before the U.S. Congress House Subcommittee on Labor, Health and Human Services and Education, April 12, 1983.

9. Drug Abuse Policy Office, *Federal Strategy for Prevention of Drug Abuse and Drug Trafficking*, 1982 (Washington, D.C.: The White House, Drug Abuse Policy Office, 1982), pp. 55-56.

10. National Institute on Alcohol Abuse and Alcoholism, *Third Special Report*, p. xi (percentages of problem drinking applied to 1982 population estimates.)

11. Neil Munch and J. Lau, *Alcoholic State Transition Dynamics (ASTD) Model of Drinking and Problem Drinking by U.S. Adults, Age 18 and Older Using 1976 Data* (Gaithersburg, Md.: Alcohol Epidemiologic Data System, April, 1980), p. 6.

12. "Alcohol Abuse and Dependence," *The Alcoholism Report*, Oct. 31, 1983, p. 7.

13. National Institute on Alcohol Abuse and Alcoholism, *Third Special Report*, p. xi.

14. National Center for Health Statistics, "Advance Report of Final Mortality Statistics, 1980," *Monthly Vital Statistics Report*, Aug. 11, 1983, pp. 19-21.

15. National Safety Council, 1982 Motor Vehicle Fatalities.

16. National Institute on Alcohol Abuse and Alcoholism, *Fourth Special Report to the U.S. Congress on Alcohol and Health*, (Rockville, Md.: National Institute on Alcohol Abuse and Alcoholism, Alcohol, Drug Abuse and Mental Health Administration, January, 1981), p. 6.

17. Office of Alcohol Countermeasures, *Facts on Alcohol and Highway Safety* (Washington, D.C.: U.S. Department of Transportation, Office of Alcohol Countermeasures, Aug. 1, 1983) pp. 4-5.

18. National Institute on Alcohol Abuse and Alcoholism. *Fourth Special Report*, p. 6.

19. Ibid, p. 6.

20. National Center for Health Statistics, "Advance Report of Final Mortality Statistics, 1980." National Safety Council, 1982 Motor Vehicle Fatalities. National Institute for Alcohol Abuse and Alcoholism, Fourth Special Report to U.S. Congress on Alcohol and Health, p. 6., 84. Alvin M. Cruze et. al., *Economic Costs to Society of Alcohol and Drug Abuse and Mental Illness — 1977* (Rockville, Md.: Alcohol, Drug Abuse and Mental Health Administration, October, 1981), p. A-4.

21. American Hospital Association, "Policy and Statement — Admission to General Hospitals of Patients with Alcohol and Other Drug Problems," (Chicago, Ill.: American Hospital Association, 1983).

22. Joseph A. Califano Jr., *The 1982 Report on Drug Abuse and Alcoholism* (New York: Warner Books, 1982), pp. 160-161.

23. "Hospitalized Hide Alcoholism Says Study," *Alcoholism*, January-February, 1982, p. 61.

24. Alan Bayer, *A Health Planner's Guide to Planning and Reviewing Alcoholism Services: Selected Readings* (Bethesda, Md.: Alpha Center for Health Planning, Oct. 1, 1980), p. 71.

25. Ibid., pp. 82-84.

26. Michael J. Eckardt et. al., "Health Hazards Associated with Alcohol Consumption," *Journal of the American Medical Association*, 246, No. 6 (Aug. 7, 1981), 648-666.

27. Kenneth R. Jones and Thomas R. Vischi, "Impact of Alcohol, Drug Abuse and Mental Health Treatment on Medical Care Utilization: A Review of the Research Literature," *Medical Care*, 17, No. 2 Supplement (December, 1979).

28. Blue Cross of Greater Philadelphia, *Joint Health Cost Containment Program Utilization Report*, (Philadelphia, Pa.: Blue Cross of Greater Philadelphia, September, 1981), p. 9.

29. National Institute on Alcohol Abuse and Alcoholism, *Fourth Special Report*, p. 92.

30. M. Strauss, R. Gellis and S. Steinmetz, *Behind Closed Doors* (New York: Doubleday & Company, Inc., 1980). (The figure of 16 percent prevalence of violent acts among couples cited in the book is applied to U.S. Census Bureau's 1982 estimate of the number of married couples in the United States.)
American Humane Association. *Annual Report 1981 — Highlights of Official Child Neglect and Abuse Reporting.* (Alcohol abuse plays a role in one-third child abuse cases.)

31. Federal Bureau of Investigation, *Uniform Crime Reports* (Washington, D.C.: U.S. Department of Justice, Federal Bureau of Investigation, 1982).

32. J.L. Francek, "Gauge Programs by Tough Standards," *Focus on Alcohol and Drug Issues*, (March-April, 1980), p. 6.

33. William Dunkin, telephone interview at the National Council on Alcoholism, June 11, 1981.

34. Califano Jr., *The 1982 Report on Drug Abuse and Alcoholism*, p. 159.

35. National Institute on Alcohol Abuse and Alcoholism, *Fourth Special Report*, p. 137.

36. National Institute on Alcohol Abuse and Alcoholism, *National Drug and Alcoholism Treatment Utilization Survey, Comprehensive Report* (Rockville, Md.: National Institute on Alcohol Abuse and Alcoholism, Alcohol, Drug Abuse and Mental Health Administration, September, 1983), p. 72.

37. Ralph Berry et. al., *The Economic Cost of Alcohol Abuse—1975* (Brookline, Mass.: Policy Analysis Inc., 1977).

38. Cruze et. al., *Economic Costs to Society of Alcohol and Drug Abuse and Mental Illness—1977*, p. A-4.

39. Office of Technology Assessment, *The Effectiveness and Costs of Alcoholism Treatment*, p. 61.

40. National Institute on Alcohol Abuse and Alcoholism, *National Drug and Alcoholism Treatment Utilization Survey*, p. 40.

41. Cruze, *Economic Costs to Society*, pp. A-34, A-38, A-45.

42. National Center for Health Statistics, "Advance Report of Final Mortality Statistics, 1980," pp. 19-21.

43. Munch and Lau, *Alcoholic State Transition Dynamics*, p. 6.

44. National Center for Health Statistics, "Prevalence of Published Chronic Conditions, Rates by Sex and Age: United States, 1981" (unpublished data from the National Health Interview Survey).

45. American Cancer Society, *1983 Cancer Facts and Figures* (New York: American Cancer Society, 1982), p. 3.

46. National Center for Health Statistics, "Tables and Charts for Sex Differences in Mortality and Morbidity: Some Aspects of the Economic Burden." Prepared by Dorothy P. Rice, Dec. 4, 1981.

47. Health Care Financing Administration, Bureau of Data Management and Strategy, "Hospital Average Charges and Length of Stay for Diagnosis Related Groups, 20 Percent Sample of Medicare Patients in 5,853 Acute Care Hospitals in The Nation During Calendar Year, 1981."

48. Alcohol, Drug Abuse and Mental Health Administration, Alcohol Epidemiologic Data System, "Table 1: Health Research Dollars in Relation to Economic Cost" (1981).

49. National Institutes of Health, *Data Book*, 1982.

50. National Institute on Alcohol Abuse and Alcoholism, *National Drug and Alcoholism Treatment Utilization Survey*, p. 38.

51. Robert M. Gibson, Daniel R. Waldo and Katharine R. Levit, "National Health Expenditures, 1982," *Health Care Financing Review* 5 (1983):1.

52. National Institute on Alcohol Abuse and Alcoholism, *National Drug and Alcoholism Treatment Utilization Survey*, p. 62.

53. Gibson, "National Health Expenditures, 1982," p. 3.

54. National Institute on Alcohol Abuse and Alcoholism, *National Drug and Alcoholism Treatment Utilization Survey*, p. 39.

55. Gibson, "National Health Expenditures, 1982," p. 7.

56. National Institute on Alcohol Abuse and Alcoholism, *National Drug and Alcoholism Treatment Utilization Survey*, p. 40.

57. Ibid., pp. 62-64.

58. Henry W. Blair, *The Temperance Movement* (Boston, Mass.: The William E. Smythe Company, 1888).

59. Paul Ohliger, "Intervention — The Newest Wrinkle in Alcoholism," *Orange County Medical Association Bulletin*, January, 1978.

60. National Association of State Alcohol and Drug Abuse Directors, "Private Health Insurance Coverage for Alcoholism and Drug Dependency Treatment Services: State Legislation That Mandates Benefits or The Offering of Benefits For Purchase" (Washington, D.C. National Association of State Alcohol and Drug Abuse Directors, July, 1983).

61. New Mexico, An Act Relating to Insurance; Providing for Alcohol Dependency Coverage, Senate Bill 79, 36th Leg., 1st sess., 1983.

62. Blue Cross and Blue Shield Association, *Substance Abuse Treatment Benefits* (Chicago: Blue Cross and Blue Shield Association, 1983), p. 114.

63. John Krizay and Edward Carels, *An Analysis of Insurance Coverage for Alcoholism in America* (Newport Beach, Calif.: CareInstitute, 1983).

64. Office of Technology Assessment, *The Effectiveness and Costs of Alcoholism Treatment*, p. 4.

65. Christopher J. Zook and Francis D. Moore, "High-Cost Users of Medical Care," *The New England Journal of Medicine* 302 No. 18 (1980):996-1002.

66. Christopher J. Zook, Sheila Flanigan Savickis and Francis D. Moore, "Repeated Hospitalization for the Same Disease: A Multiplier of National Health Costs," *Milbank Memorial Fund Quarterly/Health and Society* 58, No. 3 (1980): 454-471.

67. Jones, "Impact of Alcohol, Drug Abuse and Mental Health treatment on Medical Care Utilizaton: A Review of the Research Literature," p. 3.

68. National Institute on Alcohol Abuse and Alcoholism, *Development of Cost Simulation Study of Alcoholism Insurance* (Rockville, Md.: National Institute on Alcohol Abuse and Alcoholism, Alcohol, Drug Abuse and Mental Health Administration, May, 1983).

69. Presidential Commission on Drunk Driving. *Final Report* (November, 1983).

70. Jerry Spicer, Leslie R. Nyberg, Thomas R. McKenna, *Apples and Oranges* (Minneapolis: Hazelden Foundation, March, 1981), pp. 19-20.

71. Norman G. Hoffmann and Carol A. Belille, *Chemical Abuse/Addiction Treatment Outcome Registry, 1982 Report* (St. Paul, Minn., St. Paul-Ramsey Medical Education and Research Foundation, 1982), p. 45.

72. "Alcoholic Beverage Ad Spending Exceeds $1 Billion on 12 Percent Increase," *Impact* 12, No. 11 (1982).

About the Author

Professor Rashi Fein received his doctorate from The Johns Hopkins University in 1956. Subsequently, he began a distinguished professional career which has included positions on President Truman's Commission of the Health Needs of the Nation and President Kennedy's Council of Economic Advisors; membership in the Institute of Medicine of the National Academy of Sciences; and numerous awards as a scholar and lecturer, including a World Health Organization Traveling Fellowship.

In the fall of 1968, Dr. Fein came to Harvard University as Professor of the Economics of Medicine at Harvard Medical School and as member of the Department of Social Medicine and Health Policy.

Among Professor Fein's many and varied published works are *The Doctor Shortage, An Economic Diagnosis,* 1967, and *A Right to Health: The Problem of Access to Primary Care,* written with Charles Lewis and David Mechanic, 1976.